Trump-Proof Your Business

BILL BISHOP

Copyright © 2017 Bill Bishop
All rights reserved.
ISBN-13: 978-1542768085
ISBN-10: 154276808X

DEDICATION

To my father Arthur Bishop
and my grandfather Billy Bishop,
two warriors and entrepreneurs,
who defended our democracy in the two world wars,
and came home to build great businesses.

CHAPTER 1

MY ALTERNATIVE INAUGURAL ADDRESS

I've always dreamed of being President so when I heard Donald Trump deliver his inaugural address on January 20th, 2017, I thought, you know, I think I could improve on that. So I changed a few words, just a few, and came up with an alternative inaugural address.

I sent this revised speech to my business associates, about 1,200 people on my email list. It was a bit of a risk because I don't normally mix business with politics, but this didn't seem like normal times.

The response was overwhelmingly positive. Every business person who responded thought my inaugural speech was better than Trump's. "I wish he had said that instead," an insurance broker wrote. "I think your speech makes more sense," an IT consultant responded. "I would have voted for you Bill," a factory owner proclaimed.

The response surprised me because I thought most business owners would be Trump supporters, but that didn't seem to be the case. Only one person sent me a nasty response: "Keep your comments to yourself," she said. But all the rest were critical of President Trump and his plans for the economy. "These are regressive ideas that are going to hurt my business and the US and global economy," was the general consensus.

Then my alternative inaugural address went viral. Business owners forwarded, posted and retweeted it to their friends and associates. Suddenly we had a bit of movement going: Business people who oppose what Trump is doing, and planning to do, to the economy. Business people who believe in free trade, capitalism and entrepreneurship, and don't think the President, or any other government person or agency should be trying to mico-manage the economy and the marketplace.

All of this was very surprising and disorienting. Now we have a Republican President and party who are anti-free trade and a Democratic party that is pro-free trade. We now have a Republican President who thinks it's okay to dictate how and where companies operate. A President who plans to impose tariffs and other trade barriers that will restrict the flow of commerce. Have we gone down a rabbit hole?

As a writer, speaker and coach to entrepreneurs I could have let all of this pass. I've made a nice sum of money over the past 30 years. I could just retreat to my cabin in the woods and chop firewood for four years. But that didn't seem right. My passion is helping entrepreneurs come up with innovative BIG Ideas, and it became very apparent that they need a game plan for both survival and success under the regressive economic policies of the Trump administration.

They need to know how to build and grow their business when so much is so unclear and so uncertain. They also need to take into account more than just the machinations of Trump, they also have to plan for disruptions from new technologies, new kinds of competitors, and other potential changes in market conditions.

So I wrote this book: *Trump-Proof Your Business*. I'm going to show you how to play your cards right under a Trump administration. So instead of sitting back and waiting for something bad to happen, you're going to use proactive strategies to succeed no matter what Trump does or doesn't do.

In the upcoming chapters, I will also share with you my vision for the future, which I contend will happen no matter what President Trump does. I believe new market forces, that are unprecedented in human history, will be a tsunami that will dwarf the wave of Donald Trump during his four years in office. Whatever policies he puts in place, they will be no match for the new marketplace that is emerging.

So get ready for an exciting, uplifting and positive read. The next four years are going to be the best ever!

******

I almost forget… You are probably wondering about that alternative inaugural address. Well here it is, unabridged and uncensored:

PRESIDENT BISHOP: Chief Justice Roberts, President Carter, President Clinton, President Bush, President Obama, fellow Americans and people of the world, thank you.

(APPLAUSE)

We, the citizens of America, are now joined in a great national effort to continue building on the last eight years of job growth since the recession caused by the

financial collapse of 2008.
(APPLAUSE)

Together, we will continue the growth of the American and global economy for many, many years to come. We will face challenges, we will confront hardships, but we will get the job done.

Every four years, we gather on these steps to carry out the orderly and peaceful transfer of power, and we are grateful to President Obama and First Lady Michelle Obama for their gracious aid throughout this transition. They have been magnificent. Thank you.
(APPLAUSE)

Today's ceremony, however, has very special meaning because today, we are not merely transferring power from one administration to another or from one party to another, but we are transferring power from the people who ran the "old factory" industrial economy to those who are building the "new factory" information-based and idea economy.
(APPLAUSE)

For too long, a small group of old factory special interests have controlled our economy and political system. These industrial-minded business people flourished, but the average people did not share in its wealth. A small group prospered, but the jobs left and the factories closed when they became obsolete in today's new factory marketplace. These old factory interests protected themselves, but not the average citizens of our country. Their victories have not been your victories. Their triumphs have not been your triumphs. And while they celebrated, there was little to celebrate for struggling families all across our land.

(APPLAUSE)

That all changes starting right here and right now because this moment is your moment, it belongs to people who embrace the new factory economy. This economy has a great future. It involves things like the sharing economy, driver-less cars, machine learning computers, robotic manufacturing, 3D printing, bio-engineering, nano-technology, alternative energy production, and a host of other technologies just around the bend. The key point is: To make America great again, we need to look forward not backward.

(APPLAUSE)

We need to accept that the old economy is obsolete. It is over. The old days of manufacturing are not coming back. Those old manufacturing jobs are not coming back. We need to create a new economy that caters to the marketplace of the future, not the past.

(APPLAUSE)

What truly matters is not which party controls our government, but whether our government is controlled by old factory interests, or by those who are interested in the future.

(APPLAUSE)

January 20th, 2017 will be remembered as the day that the American people accepted the truth about the end of the industrial revolution, and fully embraced the bright promise of an exciting new future.

(APPLAUSE)

And let it be said so we are clear. The forgotten men and women of our country will be forgotten no longer. We will help them retrain and help them develop new skills. We will make their education a priority. Instead of promising them their old job back, we will help them get new jobs that are more interesting, more creative, and most importantly, more lucrative.

(APPLAUSE)

Everyone is listening now. You came by the tens of millions to become part of an historic movement, the likes of which the world has never seen before. And this movement will be incredible as long as we are not caught up in a delusion that we can turn the clock back.

(APPLAUSE)

At the center of this movement is a crucial conviction, that our economy exists to serve its citizens. Americans want great schools for their children, safe neighborhoods for their families, and good jobs for themselves. These are just and reasonable demands of righteous people and a righteous public.

But we are not going to achieve this vision by trying to run the economy by fiat. It is not going to work if the federal government plays winners and losers by bullying companies to build factories in the US, or by imposing trade barriers which inhibit business and amount to a de facto tax.

Instead, we need to get back to what made America great in the first place: capitalism, entrepreneurism, and open markets. We have to let business people be free to build the businesses of the future.

(APPLAUSE)

For many decades, we've worked with foreign countries for the shared economic benefit of all. Since World War Two, the liberalization of trade has grown our economy more than fifty fold. It has been the greatest period of economic prosperity in the history of the world. This experience has taught us that free and fair trade is in the best interest of everyone, including and especially the United States. For if our trading partners do not prosper, we cannot hope to prosper in isolation.

(APPLAUSE)

Every year, we spend trillions and trillions of dollars on weapons and the military while America's infrastructure has fallen into disrepair and decay. We've made members of the military-industrial complex rich, while the wealth, strength and confidence of our country has dissipated over the horizon.

And because the industrial revolution is over, and the new factory economy is taking its place, many factories shuttered and left our shores, while millions and millions of American workers have been left behind.

In addition, because we do not tax the wealthy enough, and allow them to dodge taxes overseas, the wealth of our middle class has been ripped from their homes and then redistributed all across the world.

But that is the past. And now, we are looking only to the future.
    (APPLAUSE)

We assembled here today are issuing a new decree to be heard in every city, in every foreign capital, and in every hall of power. From this day forward, a new vision will govern our land. From this day forward, America is going to embrace and lead the development of the new factory economy. We are going to build smart factories, expand the knowledge economy, and encourage the emergence of new kinds of business and opportunities. And we are going to make sure everyone benefits, not just a few people at the top by building a more robust social safety net, including government-funded healthcare. Because we know that a strong safety net gives people the security and confidence to take risks and become entrepreneurs.

(APPLAUSE)

Every decision on trade, on taxes, on immigration, on foreign affairs will be made to benefit everyone: both Americans, and everyone around the globe. We must protect our planet from the ravages of climate change by making our products more efficiently in ways that do not harm the environment.

(APPLAUSE)

Protecting our environment will lead to greater prosperity and strength. I will fight for the health of the planet, for peace and prosperity with every breath in my body and I will never ever let you down.

(APPLAUSE)

We the citizens of the world will have well-being again, well-being like never before.

(APPLAUSE)

We will bring back health, well-being and peace. We will bring back our respect for each and every person on the earth. We will bring back our goodwill. And we will bring back our dreams.

(APPLAUSE)

We will build a new information infrastructure, new smart grids and new energy systems, new ways to build greater wealth using less resources, while protecting the environment all across our wonderful nation. We will get our people off welfare and back to work in the new factory economy, rebuilding our country with American brains and American hearts.

(APPLAUSE)

We will follow two simple rules; be kind to each other, and work towards the common good of everyone on the planet.

(APPLAUSE)

We will seek friendship and goodwill with the nations of the world, but we do so with the understanding that it is smart to keep in mind the common good. We do not seek to impose our way of life on anyone, but rather to let it shine as an example. We will shine for everyone to follow.

(APPLAUSE)

At the bedrock of our politics will be an allegiance to all the people of the United States of America, everyone, no matter who they are or where they come from. We will rediscover the need to help each other. When you open your heart to loving-kindness, there is no room for prejudice, hatred, or greed.

(APPLAUSE)

The Bible tells us how good and pleasant it is when all of God's people live together in harmony. We must speak our minds openly, debate our disagreements honestly, but always pursue the common good. When America lives by its highest values, America is a great leader.

(APPLAUSE)

There should be no fear. We are protected and we will always be protected by our democracy. As long as we stand up for our rights, no authoritarian leader, either foreign or domestic can undermine us.

(APPLAUSE)

Finally, we must think big and dream even bigger. In America, we understand that a nation is only thriving as long as it is looking forward to the future. We will no longer accept politicians who use old factory thinking, constantly thinking about the past.

(APPLAUSE)

The time for talking about the past is over. Now arrives the hour of action.

(APPLAUSE)

Do not allow anyone to tell you that it cannot be done. No challenge can match the heart and fight and spirit of America. We will not fail. Our country will thrive and prosper.

We stand at the birth of a new kind of economy, the new factory economy, ready to unlock the mysteries of space, to free the earth from the miseries of disease, and to harness the energies, industries and technologies of tomorrow. A new kind of economy will stir our creativity, lift our sights and heal our divisions.

It's time to remember that old wisdom our soldiers will never forget, that whether we are black or brown or white, we are all human beings who want to be happy.

(APPLAUSE)

We all enjoy the same glorious freedoms and we believe in the importance of mutual respect, honesty, loving-kindness, and tolerance for those who are different from us.

(APPLAUSE)

And whether a child is born in the urban sprawl of Detroit or the wind-swept plains of Nebraska, they look up at the same night sky, their heart is filled with the same dreams, and they are infused with the breath of life by the same almighty creator.

(APPLAUSE)

So to all Americans in every city near and far, small and large, from mountain to mountain, from ocean to ocean, hear these words: We will help you face up to reality and take the actions that are necessary to achieve your health, happiness and prosperity, along with the health, happiness and prosperity of our fellow human beings around the globe.

(APPLAUSE)

Your voice, your hopes, and your dreams will define our global destiny. And your courage and goodness and love will forever guide us along the way.

Together, we will make the world strong again. We will make the world wealthy again. We will make the

world proud again. We will make world safe again. And yes, together we will make the world great again.
 (APPLAUSE)

Thank you. God bless you. And God bless us all, everyone.
 (APPLAUSE)

Thank you.
 (APPLAUSE)

God bless us all.

CHAPTER 2

NO TRUMP ECONOMICS

It was quite an evening recently when my wife and I played Bridge for the first time with another couple at their home. None of us knew what we were doing, but by the end of the evening we had played a few hands and felt we were getting the hang of it.

As we reviewed the rules, I found it interesting that No Trump is the most valuable thing to bid when you are trying to make your Contract. (We all laughed about that because it was the night of the inauguration.) To make No Trump, you have to have a lot of high cards from every suit, Diamonds, Spades, Hearts, and Clubs. Ideally, you and your partner are holding all of the Aces, and a bunch of Kings, and Queens. If you do, you can win a lot of points by winning your Contract with No Trump.

With this new nugget of knowledge planted in my mind, I thought it would make an excellent analogy for this book. The business objective is win by holding all of the best cards (strategy), and playing them properly (implementation), and doing with it No Trump, (in way that will succeed no matter what Trump does or doesn't do).

So with apologies to people who know a heck of a lot more about Bridge than I do, I decided to make this a theme of the book.

So let's start by looking what what's really going on. First, Donald Trump's campaign to "Make America Great Again." Frankly, I think America is an amazing country, a great country already. But what does he really mean by that? It means that he wants to bring back the manufacturing jobs that have disappeared in states like Ohio, Michigan, and Wisconsin. That sounds great, but is it really possible? Certainly he can bring back a few factories, but most of them are gone forever. Why? Because even if manufacturers were to return to the United States, most of these factories would be automated and run by computers and robots. Automation is one of those tsunami trends that Donald Trump can't control. So, sad as it may be for the people affected, all of those assembly line jobs are not coming back.

And let me put a firmer point on this. They are not coming back because of automation, not because those jobs are now in countries like China and India.

In fact, while India's manufacturing output has grown substantially since 2000, the number of people employed in manufacturing in India has dropped from 15% in 2000 to under 8% today. So you see, even in low-wage countries like India, people are losing manufacturing jobs to automation.

Two, exiting trade deals, and imposing tariffs is a sure fire way to damage the economy and put jobs at risk. As I said in my inaugural address, since the end of World War II, the liberalization of trade has fueled an incredible increase in prosperity around the world. And by increasing the prosperity of its trading partners, the United States has prospered. We must remember that the United States has the largest economy and the highest per capita income. So it's hard to make a case that the United States has truly suffered under these trade deals.

So what happens when the US exits trade deals like the TPP and NAFTA, and starts to impose tariffs? For starters, US imports will become more expensive, driving up the cost of living and inflation. US exports will also suffer because other countries will simply impose their own tariffs. All the money collected on these tariffs will not fuel economic growth, but rather act as a de facto tax that will end up in government coffers. The fact is: the same people who voted for Donald Trump are the same people who shop at Walmart to pick up their Chinese manufactured products. They are not going to be happy when those products are more expensive or unavailable.

So imposing tariffs is not a good idea. What about bi-lateral trade deals? President Trump wants to do unilateral trade deals with individual countries one at a time. But is that really a good idea? If the US had signed the TPP, they would have had unfettered access to a large market, and expanded its influence in the Pacific. But now, China will step up to fill this vacuum, and expand its influence further in the region.

President Trump also thinks it is a good idea to threaten and cajole companies to stay in the United States. He threatens them with penalties and shaming if they don't do his bidding. But is this a good idea? In most cases, the companies get some kind of tax break or subsidy for staying or returning to the States. But isn't that corporate welfare? Isn't that like the centralized planning that worked so abysmally in the Soviet Union? Should the federal government under President Trump be picking winners and losers in the marketplace? How in the world can the conservatives in the Republican Party agree to this kind of government interference in the workings of the marketplace? Isn't this the kind of government overreach that the Republicans accused the Democrats of doing under Obama?

In addition to all of this, you also have the negative impact of uncertainty itself. If the government is instituting dramatic changes in how things have been done traditionally, that creates uncertainty. When the government starts doing things that are unprecedented, business owners wonder about the potential repercussions. Will these new policies make things better or worse? And if we are not sure, we humans tend to defer to caution and put the brakes on things. So it's obvious, uncertainty typically has a chilling effect on investment, consumer confidence, and risk-taking. This is bad for business.

So you tell me. Can you honestly say that the things Donald Trump is doing, and planning, will really turn out well for the economy and for your business? I might be wrong, but I'm betting that it could turn out really badly for the economy in general. And we haven't talked about the tsunami trends that Donald Trump has no control over. Those trends are going to trump anything that he might do. Let's take a look at those now.

BILL BISHOP

CHAPTER 3

TSUNAMI TRENDS THAT WILL TRUMP TRUMP

President Donald Trump boasts that his election heralded a wave of change never seen before in human history. Okay. Let's give him that bit of hyperbole. But there is a number of tsunami trends that will make his wave look very small indeed.

Let's start with automation. As we examined in the last chapter, automation is a trend in manufacturing around the world. Factories are becoming more productive and efficient, and less filled with people. The joke goes: In the factory of the future, there will no workers, just a night watchman and a dog. The man will be there to turn the lights on and off, and the dog will be there to keep an eye on the man.

So that's the way it's going. We are witnessing the end of low-skilled manufacturing jobs. The robots and computers are taking over. It is no different than the decline of agriculture jobs due to the industrial revolution. As machines automated agriculture, we were able to produce more food with less people. Now we are able to produce more stuff with less people.

So the people who worked in the factories need to do something else for their work. Under current conditions, they are either unemployed or working at low-wage services jobs. No wonder they were angry during the election campaign.

But let's face facts. Only a handful of them will find new jobs in manufacturing. It's just isn't going to happen. And it seems a special brand of cruelty to hold out that hope.

So what's the answer? The people displaced by automation need to be retrained to do other things. We will get into what these jobs might look like in an upcoming chapter.

Furthermore, if you think automation has been disruptive already, you ain't seen nothing yet. In the coming years, more and more jobs will be eliminated through automation. We are looking at driver-less trucks (no more truck drivers), driver-less cars (no more taxi drivers), not to mention robot waiters, robot nurses (they already have them in Japan), and even automated financial advisers (called robo-advisers). It has been estimated that more 90% of today's jobs will be obsolete by the year 2025.

So that's scary.

Now let's turn to another trend that few people are talking about: machine learning computers. It used to be that you programed computers to do a function like word-processing or video-sharing. But now they are programming computers to learn. Using what is called *machine learning algorithms*, computer programmers give computers the ability to learn. That means that every second, every minute, and every day, without rest, these computers are getting smarter and more knowledgeable. That means that every day they can do things better, and do things that they never did before. They just keep learning.

Here's a few examples that will make your hair stand on end. Remember the computer that beat everyone on Jeopardy? It was a learning computer. Then a machine learning computer beat the world champion at chess, and a little while later, one of these machines beat the world champion at Go, considered to be the hardest game in the world.

But that's not all. Google has a machine learning computer. It's called Google Brain. The geniuses at Google had been building Google Brain for a while, and in November 2016, they decided to attach

Goggle Translate to it. That's the function on Google that translates Chinese to English or French to Russian. Up to that point the quality of the translation had been fairly low compared to what a professional translator could do. But Google Brain was a fast learner. In the first day, the quality of the translations improved more than had been achieved in ten years using the old system. Ten years improvement in one day! I haven't heard what happened on the second day, but it was probably an even greater increase in translation quality.

Is your hair standing on end yet? Well get ready for this. In India, a telemarketing company is using a super-computer equipped with a machine learning algorithm. It is able to receive calls from around the world, and answer questions in multiple languages, similar to Siri on your Apple phone. This single computer has already replaced 25,000 telemarketing jobs, and the company predicts that it will ultimately replace 25 million workers within a few years. That's just one computer!

This is one heck of tsunami trend. I'm wondering. Does the Trump administration have a plan to create new jobs displaced by machine learning algorithms?

But that's not all.

We will also witness exponential progress in medical technologies, genetic engineering, big data analytics, the Internet of Things, alternative green energy production, virtual reality, and 3D printing. We will also see a further expansion of the sharing economy, which will further disrupt traditional jobs.

I will also add another category of potential disruption called Other. I don't know what it will be, but it's a safe bet to assume that some new technology currently unknown and unexpected will emerge during the Trump administration, something that will rock their world and ours.

The last key tsunami trend that will eclipse the efforts of the Trump administration is globalization. Try as he might, Trump cannot stop the world from becoming more inter-connected. As more value becomes intangible in the form of big data, software, design, apps, and online services, the economy will naturally become more global where traditional border patrols and customs officers become irrelevant. In a world where value streams around the world at light speed, building a big wall on the Mexican border seems almost funny. It also makes the imposition of trade barriers and tariffs irrelevant. If someone in the US wants to buy a software program or a 3D printer design made in Mexico, none of Trump's border guards will ever know about the transaction. And as I will explain in the next chapter, based on the incentive-creativity of the marketplace, entrepreneurs and consumers will figure out how to make an end run around any barriers put up by government agencies.

So look for an increase in global trade in the form of intangibles, and a decline in trade for tangibles.

Here's another example of how Trump's economic policies are anachronistic. As the capabilities of 3D printing become exponentially more powerful in the next few years, more manufacturing will not be done in traditional factories, and then shipped across borders. It will be done in your office, your home, or just around the corner at a 3D printing house. (I have one already just around the block from my office). You will be able to manufacture just about anything on a 3D printer: clothes, shoes, electronics, household goods, jewelry, and replacement parts for equipment. You will be able to have a car 3D printed, and even a house. (They have already built a house with a 3D printer in Japan).

The emergence of technology like 3D printers means that value will be able to move across borders and the government will have no way to stop it or tax it. Why? Because most of the value will be created in the design of the product and the software used to run the printer. This can be produced by anyone anywhere. For example, you might pay someone in China for the design of your favorite shoes and then print them on a 3D printer you keep in your garage. Of course, you might also design a new kind of lamp that someone in Argentina wants to print.

Either way, value and money will be streaming across borders at light speed with little or nothing that the authorities can do about it.

They key point is: We are on the cusp of exponential progress and change in dozens of economic sectors. This will cause massive disruption that no government will be able to control or turn back. That's because the marketplace will control what happens based on the *incentive-creativity* of consumers and producers around the world.

So let's take a look at what I mean by incentive-creativity.

BILL BISHOP

CHAPTER 4

HOW INCENTIVE-CREATIVITY WILL RUN RINGS AROUND TRUMP

In the marketplace, and life in general, humans are very creative when they have the incentive to do so. Whatever the world throws in their way, their mind uses incentives to figure out a creative solution that serves their best interests.

I learned this lesson playing in the Canadian championships in a sport called Racketlon.

I've been a competitive tennis player for more than 50 years. I was a tennis instructor in my 20s, and recently wrote a book called *Going To The Net: The Mindfulness Approach To Tennis*. So it was interesting to me when my tennis club hosted a special kind of tournament called Racketlon.

In Racketlon, you play four different racquet sports in sequence: table tennis, badminton, squash and tennis. For each of your matches with an opponent, you play each sport up to 21 points.

As a tennis player, I knew that I would get most of my points on tennis. I figured I could do well in the other sports too, but I knew I had to win the tennis by a large margin to prevail.

After a series of matches in the Canadian Racetlon championships, I found myself in the over-45 seniors final. The matches leading up to the final had been relatively easy, but I knew the final would be a challenge because my opponent was a world-class badminton player.

In table tennis, I won 21-18. In badminton I lost 1-21. In squash, I won 21-17. So (if you do the math) going into the tennis round, I had to win 21-7 or better to become champion. That didn't seem like too much of a challenge, but unfortunately I only won 21-10, so I had to settle for runner-up.

I was perfectly happy with my results, but then I noticed something interesting. In all of the categories, A,B,C and Seniors, male and female, the good badminton players all won the championships. Not one tennis, squash or table tennis players came out on top.

I concluded that badminton players have an advantage in Racketlon for a specific reason; it's very hard to get a lot of points against a pro badminton player if you are an amateur. They can easily beat you 21-0 because there are very few unforced errors. However, it's very hard for a pro tennis player to win 21-0 because there are more unforced errors in tennis. Even the best player in the world can miss an easy shot or double fault on the serve.

At the tournament I didn't complain about this issue. I didn't want to look like a sore loser. But over the next few years, I noticed something interesting. The Racketlon tournaments attracted more and more badminton players, and less players from the other sports. And within a few years, the sport was dominated by badminton players.

This is an example of incentive-creativity. In any game, the players quickly grasp the underlying incentives and then use their creativity to exploit it. So in Racketlon, there was a greater incentive for the badminton players to participate, and less incentive for the other sport players. The unspoken skew of the game created a un-intended outcome.

Consumers are very adept at incentive-creativity. If your city starts to meter your water consumption, you have an incentive to get creative. Instead of running the tap continuously while you brush your teeth, you only run it to rinse. If the price of electricity goes up, you automate your lighting and install more energy-efficient LED bulbs.

Entrepreneurs and corporations are also hardwired for incentive-creativity. When conditions change in the marketplace, they quickly figure out the incentives and make creative moves. Sometimes, this results in unintended consequences.

For example, after the Exxon Valdes oil spill, coastal US states enacted stricter regulations and fines for oil spills. This gave big oil companies the incentive to download the risk of transporting crude to third-party companies. This lowered the liability risk for the oil producer, but actually increased the risk of an oil spill because the safety standards of the contractors were often much lower.

Consider rent controls. The government decides to control rents so that housing is less expensive for its citizens, but this undermines the incentive of developers and landlords, leading to a decline in the availability of affordable housing. Or consider the too-big-to-fail problem. If the government promises to bail out big banks if they falter, then the big banks are incentivized to take even more risk, thereby increasing the likelihood of a default. Incentive-creativity has its upsides and its downsides. But in this context—trump-proofing your business—we want to take a positive look at things.

So let's assume that President Trump does everything he promised. Let's even give him credit for keeping all of his campaign promises. Bravo! Let's assume President Trump does these things:

- Drops out of or renegotiates all US trade deals including TPP, NAFTA and even GATT;
- Imposes a 35% tariff on all goods coming into the US;
- Encourages a Buy-American attitude;
- Spends trillions on infrastructure projects;
- Builds a wall between the US and Mexico;
- Curtails immigration into the US;
- Compels companies to manufacture in the United States either by bullying or through tax incentives;
- Imposes other unforeseen economic policies of a similar nature.

If President Trump does what he promised, and it appears that he will, what will you do about it? If you are smart, and don't stick your head in the sand, you will use your incentive-creativity. You will look at how your incentives have changed and start getting creative about what to do.

To help you with this, here are 12 strategies to Trump-Proof your business. Each are incentive-creativity responses to Donald's Trump's policies.

The 12 Trump-Proof Business Strategies

1. Shift from tangibles to intangibles
2. Download risk
3. Convert overhead from fixed to variable
4. Exit business ventures that are highly regulated by government or industry
5. Work remotely with suppliers and freelancers around the world
6. Create value based on what you know (as an expert) and less on what you do (as a worker)
7. Focus first on who you want to help, rather than on what you sell (product) or do (service)
8. Be prepared to doing anything to help your customers, even if it falls outside your current skill-set, capabilities or industry
9. Create value that achieves better results, and enhances well-being, using *less* resources
10. Replace physical travel with virtual meetings
11. Focus first on your intentions, rather than success or failure
12. Stop letting the media—both mainstream, alt-right, and fake—determine your moods, thoughts, and actions

Bonus 13: Use New Factory Thinking

CHAPTER 5

THE 12 TRUMP-PROOF BUSINESS STRATEGIES

The concept of incentive-creativity is very useful in this time of economic uncertainty and rapid change. It empowers you. Yes, the President and his administration are very powerful, but there is nothing more powerful than consumers and companies acting creatively based on their incentives. Like it or not, the marketplace is the most powerful force on earth.

So when President Trump changes something fundamental in the economy, the marketplace will get to work immediately. It will calculate its incentives and then quickly take creative actions that best serve its self-interest.

This is the great lesson. When someone takes an action, there is an opposite and equal reaction. When President Trump takes a action, you and your company can take an opposite and equal reaction.

You don't have to be a victim or a passive by-stander. You can take action. In fact, you can't do anything else. Your incentive-creativity will compel you.

So let's go over those incentives again from the last chapter, and look at them as Trump-Proof strategies for success in this new era.

1. Shift from tangibles to intangibles

Donald Trump's obsession with manufacturing is, of course, political, and not grounded in an understanding of where the economy and the marketplace is headed. Let's give him credit for trying to take care of the people who got him elected. But jobs in the manufacturing sector will continue to decline as a percentage of overall employment.

The economy is headed in another direction, away from tangible value—things you can hold in your hands—to intangible value, things that are invisible. We are moving into an economy based on knowledge, ideas, and caring (KIR), value that humans can do better than computers.

Begin by acknowledging that you and your company are an expert in something. You aren't just a supplier of a product, or a provider of a service, you know things that could be very valuable to someone. For example, a security alarm installer produced an educational video and booklet that explained how to set up a security system in a storage facility. This simple knowledge product made the author over a million dollars.

So what do you know that could be valuable to someone else? How could you convert that knowledge into intellectual property?

Second, what ideas do you have for doing something better? You might think that you don't have any ideas, but that's just not true. But you may be so busy slogging away in your work to step back and come up with creative solutions for problems. For example, I saw that Donald Trump might pose a problem for business owners so I came up with the idea for this book. What problems do you see that are not being addressed? Brainstorm some ideas on how to solve them.

Then we get to caring. This is the most important tangible value of all. You have to care about others to be successful in this marketplace. You can't just try to sell something. Your prospects and customers have to feel that you care about them. In addition, if you truly care about people there are unlimited opportunities to help them with their three biggest concerns: safety, fulfillment and connection.

At the base level, people want to feel safe and

secure. What could you do in that regard? My company is currently working with a firm called ATS Traffic on a program called *Vision Zero* to help communities eliminate traffic-related fatalities and serious injuries. This intangible product is helping ATS Traffic to diversify beyond its traditional tangible products (traffic signs and road safety equipment). It will also help the company expand into other countries.

The second level of intangible value is fulfillment. How can you help your customers achieve their biggest goals? Richard Harvey, one of our clients, has created something called *The Bucket List Program*. In his program, Richard helps his clients develop their bucket list (the things they want to do before they die) and then provides the financial planning advice to help them realize their dreams. In this way, Richard's business is now based on providing fulfillment, an intangible value.

The ultimate level of intangible value is connection. At our core, this is what we desire most, being connected to others. That's why it is so regressive for Donald Trump to pursue disconnection. While disconnection might appeal to people in the heat of a political campaign, it's not what they want in the long-run. So what can you do to bring people together? How can you create a community or network either on the Internet or in real life? There is a lot of money to be made by creating a community. Ask Facebook if that is working for them? Or how about LinkedIn? By building a community of 440 million members, LinkedIn was able to sell its business to Microsoft for $26 billion.

There are powerful incentives to make the transition from tangibles to intangibles in the Trump era. If trade barriers to tangible products go up, then it's in your best interest to sell intangibles that can cross borders with little or no restrictions.

2. Download risk

Why are you taking so much risk? Why are you on the hook in case something goes wrong? Often we think that is our job as entrepreneurs, to assume risk. But we are using the wrong verb. We want to *take* risks, but we don't have to *assume* risks. (Believe me, this is one thing Donald Trump has figured out).

We are entering a very risky time. The conditions of the market are going to change more rapidly and in more unpredictable ways. In this environment, you have to make sure that you don't assume any risks that are unnecessary.

For instance, I used to assume a lot of risk associated with printing. When my client wanted something printed, I received money from them and then paid the printer, making a profit on the markup. That worked great when everything went smoothly. But one time a client stiffed me for $5,000. He went broke and couldn't pay me. But I still had to pay the printer. I lost $4,000.

That's when I got a little wiser. Going forward, I got the printer to bill the client and give me a finder's fee. So if the client didn't pay, the printer was out of luck not me.

In another case, we used to host our clients' email and website accounts on our company servers. We made very little money on the services, but we had it in our heads that we should do it. But then it dawned on us that we were assuming too much risk for too little reward. What if the server went down, or we lost all of the data? We could face a huge liability. So we post-haste converted our clients over to a third-party company and eliminated the risk.

So in your case, how can you either eliminate or download risk in your business? This is a good idea anytime, but it is especially important under President Trump.

3. Convert overhead from fixed to variable

This is another trend that is being driven by market forces. As the pace of change accelerates, fixed assets have become a problem. In the old days, you could build a factory and produce the same thing for 10 or 20 years as you paid off the upfront investment. But nowadays, fixed assets are more likely to become obsolete long before the initial investment has been paid off.

The same goes for employees. The on-going cost of maintaining full time employees has become, unfortunately, prohibitive for many companies. While it sounds good for President Trump to say that he wants to create high-wage full-time jobs, there has to be entrepreneurs out there with the incentive to provide them.

So what do you do in your case? It doesn't mean that you should ditch all of your fixed assets, and all of your full time employees, but you might consider incorporating more variable overhead into your operation. Variable overhead is great because you only pay for it when you need it. Instead of being viewed as a cost, variable overhead is viewed as an investment that always make you money.

4. Exit business ventures that are highly regulated by government or industry

President Trump says he hates regulations that restrict business operations. One business woman, who objected to my rewriting of Trump's speech, said that she supported the new President because he will stop government "over-reach" into her business. I told her I was definitely not a big fan of government regulation in my business either, and I suggested that she take her aversion even further: Extricate herself from any business venture that is highly regulated either by the government or by industry regulators. You see, regulation doesn't just come from government, it also comes from your industry. Somehow, we feel that they are different—government regulations bad, industry regulations, necessary. We feel that way sometimes because we benefit from "regulatory capture" that protects us from outside competitors or other threats.

So let's face it, we don't always hate regulations. I'm still a fan of food inspections and traffic lights. But generally speaking, regulations are a total drag if you run a business, so why put up with them at all?

That's why I recommend you create an escape plan. How could you redesign your business so you no longer run the risk of having inspectors, auditors and other people with clipboards rummaging through your filing cabinets?

One of my clients got out from under the thumb of the regulators in the financial service industry. Faced with declining commissions on regulated financial products, he decided to create a different kind of business to help people with their financial situation. And now, because he doesn't sell financial products, he is seen as a more objective advisor (he charges people a fee for his advice) he is also operating outside the jurisdiction of the regulators. Added bonus: His blood pressure has gone down. So put your thinking cap on. What kind of business could you build that is no longer subject to industry or government regulations?

Now you might think: Why do I need to do that if Trump is going to do away with regulations? Because it is a bunch of hogwash. There is no government in the world that doesn't regulate something. If they eliminate one set of regulations they eventually come in with a new set. They can't help themselves. Once they get into power, governments like to control things. It's the whole point of getting into power. You can already see this with Trump. He is ordering companies around, changing trade deals, and building walls. These are regulations, just different regulations. So do what you can to extricate yourself from the whole mess.

5. Work remotely with suppliers and freelancers around the world

Here is where Donald Trump is going in completely the wrong direction. He is creating an immigration chill in America. Trump has spread the idea that immigrants are a problem. That they take jobs away from Americans. This kind of rhetoric will have its repercussions. In addition, he is banning immigration from terrorist-prone countries. Now this actually sounds wise. We should be careful not to let in any terrorists. I get that. A ban maybe a good idea on some level. But it creates that chill again. This means that potential immigrants from other countries—smart, talented and well-meaning people—are going to think twice about coming to America. Can you blame them? How do they know if they will be welcomed and treated kindly. Maybe America is no longer a place they want to come to.

So what do you do in your business under these conditions? The fact is: there is a shortage of skilled talent in many US industries. These industries need new immigrants. So what's the answer? I suggest that you start working remotely with talented people around the world. Build a virtual team with people from other countries. What's Donald Trump going to do about that? He can't do anything. You are just trying to build the best team possible so you can provide the maximum value possible. Why would a Republican President have a problem with that?

I've used this strategy to great effect. I work with writers, designers, software engineers, translators, and host of other incredible professionals from over 12 different countries. I don't even think any more about how extraordinary it is. It's just a great way to run a business.

So once again, Donald Trump's policies are generally irrelevant if you design your business the right way.

6. Create value based on what you know (as an expert) and less on what you do (as a worker)

President Trump and his administration are fixated on factories and assembly-line workers. Good for them! There will always be a segment of the economy that will fit that category. But it will be declining category.

In addition, there is this meme out there that we have entered a post-expert world. No one respects experts anymore. After all, why bother using someone who knows what they are doing, when you can just consult the Internet and do it yourself?

But this is a delusion. We are moving into the heyday of the knowledge economy and the ascendance of the expert. As I mentioned earlier, everyone is an expert at something, they just don't see themselves that way. Maybe they think it is immodest to call themselves an expert. But this is self-defeating. The marketplace of the future will be calling out for expertise in every field of human endeavor.

The marketplace will be clamoring for experts because experts know a lot of valuable things like: How to get better results for less time, money and effort. How to avoid costly mistakes. Strategies that work best. Where to find the best resources faster and easier and for less money. How to pull together diverse elements into an integrated whole. How to turn a complex problem into a simple elegant solution.

What is descending is the demand for labor. As time goes by, your time and effort will become less valuable because it will be better performed by a robot or a learning algorithm. That's why you need to focus on what you know and teach it to others. Help them do something rather than trying to do it for them.

Packaging your expertise is also scalable. If you package up what you know—say in a book like this—you could sell a million of them while relaxing on a beach somewhere. You can't say that for your labor.

So get on this trend. Forget Trump's obsession with factories and assembly lines. That is so 20th Century—if not 19th Century.

Be the expert.

7. Focus first on who you want to help, rather than on what you sell (product) or do (service)

In addition to factories and assembly-line workers, President Trump is also thinking about products like air conditioners, cars, and farm equipment. He wants these products made in the United States. Sounds like a good idea.

But the future is not on his side once again. Companies that focus on producing a specific product—like hammers—are at risk in today's marketplace because product life cycles are incredibly short. You could have hit product today and be out of business in 12 months as the popularity of your product is eclipsed by something else. So if you build your business around a specific product—or service—you could set yourself up for disruption.

You're also vulnerable to commoditization, whereby the profit margins on your products are driven down by price-competition.

In this marketplace you need to be very flexible. You have to adopt the attitude that the marketplace creates your business. If you sell something the marketplace wants you will be successful. If you sell something the marketplace doesn't want, you will fail.

The problem here is that the marketplace is fickle. It loves you one day, and dumps you the next. Suddenly, you might find yourself with a warehouse full of hammers that nobody wants.

So don't fall in the product-first trap. Instead use the relationship-first formula. That's when you build your business around a type of customer, rather than a type of product or service.

One of my clients thanks his lucky stars that he used this way of thinking. Back in 1998, he decided to work exclusively with the owners of construction companies. When he met with a prospect he said: "I specialize in working with people like you, the owners of construction companies." This was very meaningful to these owners. They were interested to hear what Doug had to say. One of these prospects bought a $500 million life insurance policy from him.

Years later Doug commented that focusing on

the customer type was the best strategy he ever used. "It helped me get focused more clearly on my value proposition, and it gave me lots of ideas about new things I could do that were tailored specifically for their needs. It was very helpful."

So be like Doug. Stop thinking all the time about your products and services. They are a given. Start thinking more about who you are trying to help. Become an expert in helping that kind of person.

This strategy has two practical benefits. One, it future-proofs your business. No matter what President Trump does, or what other disruptions happen in the marketplace, you will be firmly anchored around a type of customer. Nothing can change that. Secondly, it means that change and disruption are now in your favor. Your new task will be to help your specific type of customer deal with change and disruption. After all that's when they are most likely to listen to, and do, new things. In fact, here's an adage to keep in mind: People buy more when things change.

So who is your customer type? Who do you want to help?

8. Be prepared to doing anything to help your customers, even if it falls outside your current skill-set, capabilities or industry.

This strategy builds on the previous one. Once you have selected your customer type, you start to think about all the ways you could help them solve their problems and achieve their goals.

The key is to be open minded. If you sell hammers to your customers, consider also selling them screw drivers. You could also sell them yoga lessons or hair loss treatments. Anything and everything is possible at this point.

This is the approach being used by companies like Amazon, Apple, Google, Facebook and UBER. They all have their primary product or service, but they have branched out into a galaxy of other value offerings. That's why Amazon, which started with books, now sells office supplies, groceries, and just about anything. That's why Apple, which started with computers, now sells music, phones, tablets, watches, and a host of other things. They have created what I call a "Value Hub". They build a hub of value around their customers, to sell them whatever they want and need. They also set a good example for another key concept. They don't worry if they make the product they are selling, or whether it fits in their existing industry category. They are willing to consider anything that their customers might want. As well, they are not thinking about competitors. They are willing to work with their competitors or sell their competitor's products, if that would be in the best interest of their customers.

Granted, this concept is not easy to implement. Our minds are wired to focus on selling our own products and to try and beat out our competitors. We feel we belong to an industry. But none of this matters to your customers. They just want what they want. They don't care what industry you belong to. If someone from outside your industry provides something better, they will flock to them. Just ask taxi drivers about UBER.

9. Create value that achieves better results, and enhances well-being, using *less* resources

President Trump and his team will never get this strategy so don't even bother telling them about it. But this is the direction the entire world economy is headed. Every day, entrepreneurs, engineers, scientists and consumers are working on a big collective project: how to get better results, and enhance well-being, using *less* resources. Remember those learning computers I talked about, and big data analytics, and the Internet of Things, and the sharing economy? Getting better results with less time, money, effort, and energy, is what these innovations are all about. They are figuring out how to heat your home with less energy. How to get from A to B in less time. How to produce a higher-quality product for less money, less people, and less effort.

Why is this? Is it because the world is being controlled by tree-hugging, climate-change-deluded liberals who want to wreck the American way of life? Hardly. It is just producers and consumers using their incentive-creativity to their advantage.

I mean: who doesn't want to save money on their energy bill? Who doesn't want to take less time to travel across town? What manufacturer doesn't want to produce their products while using less time, money and energy?

So this is your great opportunity. Think of ways that will help your customers get better results while using less resources. Help your customers achieve greater well-being by consuming less. This sounds counter-intuitive—don't we want our customers to consume more?—but more for less is what your customers want, and if you don't do it for them, they will go somewhere else.

This is another tsunami trend that Donald Trump and his cohorts don't see coming. But it is inexorable. Little by little, the demand for traditional energy, and old ways of doing things, will decline as these technologies make them obsolete. Right now, this trend is going slowly and no one is noticing, but it will speed in the coming years. Get on it!

10. Replace physical travel with virtual meetings

Under the Trump administration, travelling, especially across borders, is going to become more onerous and perhaps more dangerous. Sure, the border will be beefed up to keep out the terrorists, but that will likely slow everything down. It will also be harder to get into other countries because they will probably beef up their borders too.

I experienced this first hand in 2015 while crossing the border between India and Nepal. At that time, the two countries were having a dispute over oil, and the borders had tightened. On the Indian side of the border, there was a ten-kilometer line of trucks waiting to cross over into Nepal. It was going to take them three or four days to get across. Fortunately, it only took us a few hours to get across, but it was a long and nerve-wracking experience.

We also discovered the same problem crossing

from one state to the next within India. States in India have their own borders for commercial traffic, and it is one of the reasons why India has failed to match China in economic growth.

So you can expert that travel is going to become more tiresome, stressful and expensive under a Trump administration. That makes face to face meetings less profitable. Better to have more virtual meetings.

I've certainly made this change in my business. We do most of our business remotely, even within our city. It is just faster and easier. It is also better for the environment.

Virtual meetings also expand your horizons. You begin to realize that you can have customers and suppliers everywhere. I used to think my customers needed to be located in my city. But now, using remote meeting technology, I have clients in China, Australia, Columbia, France, and the Netherlands. And that's the big point here. Figure out how to make borders meaningless to your business. If borders are a reality in your business now, that is going to be a problem under a Trump administration. President Trump is focused on borders. The UK is focused on borders. Many other countries are doing the same. Now is the time to take them out of your company's equation for success.

11. Focus on your intentions, not results

Managing your emotions could be challenging under a Trump administration. With every tweet or presidential press conference, you could be twisted into knots wondering what it all means for your business. So we need to make sure that you have solid ground under you. That's why you need to focus on your intentions, not results.

I used to be a participant in a business coaching program. It was a good course, but it had an inherent flaw in its approach. The head coach was obsessed with *confidence*. He gave us exercises to help us boost our confidence. These exercises seemed helpful because they did indeed boost my confidence, but the effects were short lived. Within a few days, especially if something negative happened, my confidence would plummet.

Years later I realized that a focus on confidence is a fool's game. I realized that the more I worked on my confidence, the more apparent it was that I lacked confidence.

So I decided to forget about confidence. Maybe I didn't have any control over it, and the conditions that affected it. I realized that most of the conditions that affect my business and my life are completely beyond my control. I realized I needed something else to hang my hat on.

Eventually I realized that intentions are a much better anchor. No one can take your intentions away from you. No matter what happens in the marketplace, none of it will change your intentions. That's the kind of psychological anchor I needed.

With this insight, I pondered: "What are my intentions?" I realized they were very simple: "I'm trying to help people."

Since that time, I regularly remind myself about my intentions: "I'm trying to help people." This mantra has given me clarity and a sense of purpose. It has also made a focus on confidence irrelevant. It doesn't matter how I feel about my future at any point. In addition, I've given up on assessing my success based on results. In most cases I'm not in control of the results that will be achieved. There are too many variables. But I can evaluate myself on my intentions. I can ask: "Did I try to help people in that situation?" If so, I can feel I did all that I could.

So the same goes for you. Decide on your intentions. Put them into words. Keep reminding yourself what they are. So no matter what President Trump does or says, you won't get sidetracked or disoriented. You will be firmly anchored on your intentions.

12. Stop letting the media—both mainstream, alt, and fake—determine your moods, thoughts, and actions.

Nothing I dislike more than feeling that someone is jerking my chain. I hate it because I know that I am culpable in the matter. I handed them the chain and let them jerk it.

That's how I feel about the media right now—whether it is the mainstream media, the alt-right media, or the fake news crowd. The barrage of news, gossip and commentary is generally not conducive to my well-being.

Now don't get me wrong. We need to be supportive of journalists. They are a key element of our democracy (My background is in journalism). We also have an obligation to stay informed. But we need to properly manage our intake of the news. That's why I've gone on a media diet since the election. Over the inauguration weekend my wife and I had a three-day media blackout. We didn't watch the TV, listen to the radio, or read anything on the Internet. The experience was very enlightening. One, we realized that the world carried on without us. The world didn't need us. Two, we realized that we didn't need to know everything that was going on. Three, we felt more relaxed and calm. I slept much better and felt more rested.

Coming out of the media blackout also made us realize how much the media affects our moods, thoughts and actions. After 24 hours, I felt more agitated, worried, and grumpy. I was caught up again in the whole drama. I couldn't sleep.

Then I realized that my intake of the media affected my business. It stopped me from focusing on my customers and helping them. So I developed a media defense system. I took Facebook off my phone and tablet. Now I can only check Facebook on my computer. I also took the media apps off my phone. Now if I want to read the news I have to get out my iPad. I also stopped reading digital media after 9 pm, and don't take any devices to bed with me.

These measures helped. Frankly, it seems that the Trump administration is bent on scrambling our minds. I think they are trying to drive the "Liberals" and the "Dishonest Media" crazy, but this campaign will also backfire and have unintended consequences because it undermines the ability of people to focus properly on their work or make good business decisions based on reliable information.

So I hope you will join me in being media savvy under the Trump administration.

CHAPTER 6

TRUMP: AN OLD FACTORY THINKER

In my previous book *The New Factory Thinker*, I explained why the old way of thinking about business is obsolete and why a new way of thinking about business is taking its place. I called these two modes of thinking *Old Factory Thinking* and *New Factory Thinking*.

Unfortunately, the Trump administration is staffed with an army of old factory thinkers. They want to make America Great Again. The problem is the word "again." Although they might deny it, the Trump people's brains are wired for a way of thinking that is completely obsolete and totally inadequate for dealing with the realities of today's economy and marketplace.

To Trump-Proof your business, you can't follow their lead. They will lead you back to the 1950s. You need to look ahead to 2020 and beyond. To do this properly, you need to rewire your brain for new factory thinking. Here in an excerpt from my book *The New Factory Thinker* is an explanation of old factory thinking:

Old Factory Thinking Explained

When Henry Ford perfected the moving assembly line in 1913, he ushered in the modern age. Old factory thinking had reached its zenith. Up to that point, cars had been built one at a time by craftsmen, making them too pricey for the average person. Ford's assembly line changed all that. Model T Fords took only 93 minutes to assemble with a new one coming off the line every three minutes. This efficiency allowed Ford to drop the price from $825 in 1908 to $575 in 1913. Millions of people could now afford to buy his car. Even better, Ford was able to raise wages from $1.50 a day to $5.00 a day, making it easier for his own workers to buy a car as well.

The spectacular success of Ford's assembly line was an inspiration to other entrepreneurs. They studied what Ford was doing and tried to copy his methods in their business. Initially, Ford's assembly line process was directly applied to other manufactured products but it eventually influenced service businesses like restaurants and insurance companies. It also became the organizational model for other sectors such as education, healthcare, and government services. All the assembly lines in the economy then joined together into a single, integrated assembly line system. Success as a company and as an individual meant fitting into this linear system; to find your place in the machine. Whether you worked on an assembly line in a factory, taught high school, or worked at home as a housewife, your role in life was oriented around the organizing principle of the assembly line. This way of life then conditioned our minds to think of the world as an assembly line: to be an assembly line person using assembly line thinking.

Today, the vast majority of the world's people still think and act like it's 1913. And because the world has changed, they feel like strangers in a strange land. They don't know how to navigate this new landscape so they often feel frustrated, angry and scared. You might feel that way yourself. I know I did. That's why we need to deconstruct our old factory thinking. We have to make it visible and then do away with it.

So what does an assembly-line-oriented mind look like? Let's take a look at the underlying concept of an assembly line. It works like this:

1. Acquire resources from the environment or

from other organizations.

2. Assemble these resources in an efficient step-by-step process.

3. Deliver a quality product or service at a low price.

When you get it right, an assembly line is an amazing thing. You can produce millions of cars, toasters, hamburgers, life insurance policies, and handbags, and do it in less time and for less money. You can lower your prices and attract more customers, and if you're a nice employer like Henry Ford, you can raise salaries and give your productive employees big bonuses.

The assembly line economy was a wonderful innovation. It raised the standard of living for billions of people and created the modern economy we have today, but it came with an unexpected consequence. It wired our minds to see the world from an assembly line perspective. It told us to:

• Do more;
• Do things faster;
• Use more resources;
• Focus on producing and selling more products/services;
• Specialize in a product or service;

- Focus on your individual objective; and
  - Measure results quantitatively.

Old factory thinking pervaded all areas of society but it became manifest most visibly in the structure of companies. Each company was designed as an assembly line, and endeavored to fit into the overall assembly line structure of the economy. Creating and operating a business meant creating and operating an assembly line. This led to a four-stage thinking process, which I call the old factory business model. The four stages are:

1. Pick a product or service
2. Set up operations (your assembly line)
3. Make a sales pitch
4. Do transactions

1. Pick a product or service

Old factory thinkers begin with an idea for a product or service. Perhaps they want to design wedding dresses or become a cosmetics wholesaler. Or maybe they want to provide in-home eldercare services or host extreme travel in the arctic. Some of their ideas might be truly innovative and creative but they make a critical error. By defining their business around a particular product or service, they don't think about what will happen in the future when their offering no longer interests customers or when new competitors start selling the same thing. They don't take into account change or competition as inevitable factors. And because of this, they may one day regret being typecast.

The other problem with building a business around a product or service is that you unnecessarily restrict your potential. If you think you're in the hammer business, you don't contemplate selling screwdrivers. You lock yourself into a very narrow box. Theodore Levitt, a marketing professor at Harvard, diagnosed this self-limiting mentality in the 60s as "marketing myopia". He used the example of the railroad companies at the turn of the 20th Century who thought they were in the "railroad" business and didn't see the potential of branching out into automobiles, airplanes, and other transportation-related businesses. According to Levitt, this myopia caused the railroads to define themselves too narrowly, and as a result, they missed out on big opportunities for growth. Having product or service ideas is not wrong. Keep coming up with ideas to provide new kinds of value. Just don't define yourself or your business based on these products or services.

2. Set up operations

With a product or service in mind, the old factory thinker then sets out to construct an operational structure to make and deliver it. This often begins with a desk, a computer, telephone, a pad of paper and a pen. This simple start can then lead to giant factories with multi-stage assembly lines, scores of employees punching the clock, and all of the other operational paraphernalia associated with a growing enterprise such as trucks, warehouses, signage, photocopiers, and insurance.

But this focus on expanding operations is a trap. Because old factory operations are designed around a particular product or service, you restrict your ability to adapt to changes in the marketplace. If you have an assembly line to make hammers, it's not easy to start making something else. You also turn a blind eye to the potential of other things because you're emotionally and financially invested in your infrastructure. In addition, the cost of operations turns into a huge problem if your product or service becomes a commodity. As the price of your product falls, the cost of your overhead remains the same (or increases) and this takes a big bite out of your profits.

3. Make a sales pitch

Nothing epitomizes the old factory era more than the image of a door-to-door salesman peddling vacuum cleaners to apron-clad housewives in the 1950s. While the tacky glad-handing salesperson is a firmly-entrenched cultural icon that makes us chuckle, most companies today still engage in the same basic approach to sales. Once they've chosen their product or service, and built operations around it, they enter the marketplace and give a sales pitch: *Here is our great product. It's better than anything else on the market. It's got these amazing features. Here's the price. We'll give you a deal.*

In the old factory era, straight-up sales worked great. People were interested in hearing a sales pitch. They weren't being bombarded with thousands of sales messages a day. They were also more accessible because they couldn't hide behind technology like security systems and voice mail. If you knocked on their door, they would have probably answered it, and if you called them, they would have probably picked up the phone. But that's not the world we live in today. Prospects are much harder to reach because they abhor a sales pitch.

Besides being ineffective, a sales pitch mentality has other drawbacks. By focusing on the features and benefits of your product, you fail to investigate the true needs and wants of your customers. If you have a quota to sell 1,000 hammers this month, you won't ask the customer what they really want. You don't care. You don't want to discover they really want screwdrivers. You want them to buy hammers. This emphasis on your personal product (hammers) and your own goals (sell 1,000 hammers) can make you self-absorbed and uninterested in other people, and stop you from developing bigger relationships and making bigger sales.

4. Do transactions

The fourth step—do transactions—is the way old factory thinkers keep score of their success. If they sell 10,000 hammers this year, they want to sell 20,000 hammers next year. Pumping more products and services through the assembly line becomes the key driving force of the organization. All the intellectual and creative energy of the company is focused on determining one thing: how can we move more of our product? While this sounds like the right course of action, transaction-oriented goal-setting is another old factory trap because it diverts attention away from opportunities that might prove to be much more lucrative. By only thinking about how to sell hammers, you don't create other kinds of value (like screwdrivers) that might be even more profitable.

Decoding The Machine Language

This four-stage process is so engrained in our thinking we don't question it. But that's what I'm asking you to do: question it. Notice your own thought process. Is your business defined by its product or service? Are your operations built around that product or service? Do you make a sales pitch? Do you keep score by tracking transactions?

If you're honest, you'll admit you use old factory thinking. But don't worry. You're not alone. It's used by 99.9% of business people today, in every kind of business in every kind of industry. This includes manufacturers, service companies, wholesalers, and retailers. It applies equally to consumer or business-to-business-oriented companies. It also applies to most Internet-based enterprises.

The old factory business model is so ingrained in our thinking that we don't know it's there. It's like a computer's machine language. That's the deep code programmed into a computer's chip. Most people don't know about this level of programming in their computer. They're familiar with their computer's operating system (like iOS) and its individual software applications (such as Word or Excel), but they don't know about its machine language. And yet, it's the machine language that dictates the structure of the operating system and the software applications. The same is true with the old factory business model. It's been the core mental programming of all companies during the past 200 years but it's so engrained in our thinking that we don't even know it's there.

This is also the thinking used by all of the people in the Trump administration, and members of Congress on both sides of the aisle. This is the real problem with the current administration and Washington in general. It is set up to serve the interests and needs of the old factory economy, while the opportunity and future lies in the new factory economy.

Let's now turn to new factory thinking, as the ultimate way to Trump-Proof your business.

BILL BISHOP

CHAPTER 7

NEW FACTORY THINKING

It would be wonderful if President Trump could rewire his brain for new factory thinking, but I'm personally not waiting around for that to happen. Instead, I'm encouraging everyone to use this new way of thinking order to Trump-Proof their business.

The key thing to remember is this: New factory thinking is not something I cooked up. It is something I've observed coaching hundreds of entrepreneurs. I've witnessed that this way of thinking is being rewarded in the marketplace, while old factory thinking is being punished.

So here's an explanation of new factory thinking (once again an excerpt from my book *The New Factory Thinker*).

New factory thinking has five elements:

1. Specialize in one type of customer
2. Help your customers achieve a BIG Idea
3. Provide free value during the sales process
4. Enroll customers in a membership program
5. Sell products from a one-step store

1. Specialize in one type of customer

Unlike an old factory designed around a product or service, a new factory is designed around a single type of customer. For example, instead of building a business around "hammers" you could build a business around "do-it-yourselfers". The new factory is then defined not by *what* it makes and sells; it's defined based on *whom* it helps.

This customer-first perspective unshackles your mind. You are now free to think of new ways to help your customers; ways that go beyond the standard products offered in your industry. In fact, you are free to make and sell anything as long as it's considered valuable by your customers. This realization keeps your mind curious, nimble and intellectually engaged.

From an operational standpoint, this open-minded attitude means you begin each relationship with a blank slate and work through a discovery process to help your customers articulate their goals and then make a plan to achieve them. Based on what you are learning from the marketplace (i.e.

people want screwdrivers, not hammers) you're prepared to restructure your entire business if it will better assist your customers in achieving their goals.

On a deeper level, building your business around a customer type helps you escape from an egocentric worldview. Instead of your business being all about you, your business is all about others. This is not only more meaningful, it's good for business. Using the new factory model helps you align your social good intentions with the dictates of making a living, something that the old factory model often made difficult.

Building your business around a type of customer, instead of products and services, also makes sense in a fast-changing marketplace. I've seen many people tie their reputation in the marketplace to a particular product or service only to find that its popularity was fleeting. Then they had to start again by re-branding themselves (usually around another product or service). This is a bad idea in a marketplace that is constantly changing. However, if you pick the right type of customer, you never have to change it no matter what happens in the marketplace. This gives your business a strong anchor of stability that's impervious to inevitable changes in market conditions.

2. Help your customers achieve a big idea

A big idea communicates what a new factory tries to help its customers achieve, and the unique way it helps them achieve it. It's not an idea for a product or service; it's an intangible concept. Customers don't hold it in their hands, they hold it in their minds. It has two key components: the *BIG Goal* and the *Signature Solution*.

The big goal is transcendent: it's a desired outcome that transcends the small-minded benefits achieved by old factories. It's also an intention rather than a promise. You can't guarantee you'll achieve it, but you have the intention to try. Here are a few examples of big goals:

- Be ten times safer
- Be ten times more fulfilled
- Be ten times more connected
- Have 20 times more fun
- Lower your costs by 50%
- Increase sales by 300%

- Make twice the income while working 50% less time
- Lose 100 pounds in six months
- Win a gold medal at the Olympics
- Feel greater well-being using less resources

To be effective, a big goal needs to be lofty and challenging. This gets customers to take notice and get inspired about what you're trying to do. You want your potential customers to see that you're trying to help them achieve something big and significant.

Another part of the big idea is the signature solution. This is a new, more advanced approach that helps your customer achieve the big goal. It's based on your years of experience working with many customers. Over that time, you've learned what works and what doesn't, and have boiled it down to one key action, tool or strategy. For example, to help someone lose 100 pounds in six months, you might have a signature solution called *The Hopping Method*. You teach your customers to hop on one leg for an hour a day, and by doing so; they lose the 100 pounds (as long as they don't drink six beers at the same time!). Over the years, you've learned that hopping is a good way to lose weight.

Packaging a big idea provides many benefits to a new factory thinker. One, it's easy to test in the marketplace. Without investing a lot of capital, you can try the idea on a few existing customers to see if it works. If it doesn't work then you can easily pivot to an alternative idea. In this way, you can quickly ascertain the best big idea. Secondly, it's another great anchor. No matter what happens in the marketplace, your big idea doesn't need to change. For example, its unlikely people in the future won't want to lose 100 pounds in six months. Thirdly, the big idea refocuses your intellectual and creative energies. Instead of trying to figure out how to sell more products, you now focus on thinking about new ways to help your customers achieve their goals. Having a more transcendent intention, that's all about your customers, not about you, opens the closed fist of your mind.

3. Provide free value during the sales process

In order to draw prospects out of their sales-pitch bunker, new factory thinkers provide free value during the sales process. It's like giving away a free piece of chocolate in order to sell the whole box.

The immediate objective of the free value strategy is to sign up *subscribers*. You nail down a formal relationship with a prospect by getting them to sign up for a mailing list or a free service. This technique is now commonplace. Many companies offer prospects a free version of their service, either for a month, or on an on-going basis. For example, Skype provides subscribers with free telephone service. Google provides dozens of free applications, and Apple provides thousands of free apps. Their objective is to get lots of free subscribers and then convert them into paying members.

By becoming a subscriber, the person is required to give a certain amount of personal information and agree to receive some form of on-going communication. This is called *permission marketing*, a term coined by Seth Godin in his book of the same title. Eventually some of the subscribers move to the next level and become a member.

Giving free value during the sales process can take many forms. It can be a subscription to an e-mail newsletter or a free version of your product or service. It can be a certain amount of consulting time. Ideally, the free value is a facsimile or segment of the membership program (see next step) so the subscriber gets a taste of what they will experience if they become a full-fledged paying member.

The free value approach gives a new factory a huge advantage over its competitors who use traditional sales techniques. One, it's much easier to attract a prospect when you give them something for free. You don't have to spend time selling; you just give them the free sample. This speeds up the sales process and lowers your cost of sales. Additionally, providing free value gives you more leverage in the company-prospect relationship. To get the free value, the prospect must give you something: either their personal information and/or their attention. You can also dictate who gets the free value and who doesn't. Like a bouncer at a popular nightclub, you decide who gets in and who doesn't. Psychologically, by restricting access to the free value, you increase its perceived value, making it even more desirable.

Most importantly, free value helps you bring more potential customers into your world. It creates a crowd around your business and projects an aura of popularity. It also gives you a much larger group of prospects to work with and enables you to demonstrate the value you provide, rather than just talk about it. It also enables you to shed the negative image of a salesperson and be perceived instead as someone who is successful, popular and in-demand.

4. Enroll customers in a membership program

A old factory has customers, a new factory has members. Because they are part of a "program" these members have "membership consciousness." They are conscious of being part of a larger community and feel a special affiliation with the new factory. And because they have received a lot of value from the new factory—both before and after becoming a member—they're open to buying other things, even if the products and services do not fall within the original industry-parameters of the relationship. (For example, people who originally bought a computer from Apple now purchase music, telephones and apps. Amazon customers who originally bought books now buy groceries, office supplies and fitness equipment.)

The most important marketing objective of a new factory is to sign up members. If it has 2,000 members this year, it wants 4,000 members next year. To get and keep these members, it sets up a structured program packaged with a range of membership benefits. It makes it clear what members get that non-members don't get. (That's why Amex says membership has its privileges). It either charges a fee for membership, or provides it for free, in the hopes of selling products from its one-stop store (see next).

Fostering membership consciousness is important because customers today are fickle. They don't feel guilty about shopping around for the best price or jumping ship to a competitor for a better deal. But members stay put because they are imbedded in the company's eco-system. For example, my stepdaughter Robin kept exhorting me to switch from an iPhone to an Android smart phone. "It's a better phone," she said. But I told her I couldn't do it even if I wanted to because I was ensconced in the Apple eco-system. "I would have to change my whole life if I switched from Apple to Android," I said.

The most powerful reason why members become firmly attached to a new factory is because they buy into its big idea. They have a powerful "why" in their mind about why they have a relationship with the new factory (i.e. becoming 10 times safer, more fulfilled or more connected), and they realize the new factory is the only company that provides the big idea. To go to another supplier is simply not an option, either practically or emotionally.

5. Sell products and services from a one-stop store

A new factory is not tied to any particular industry. While it's old factory may have started in a traditional industry, the new factory sells products and services from multiple industries. The best current example is Apple: it sells its traditional products from the computer industry, but also sells products from the music, telephone, and movie industries.

By expanding into other industries, and selling products created by other companies, the new factory expands its potential revenue without increasing its risk profile, capital investments or fixed overhead. By sourcing outside suppliers, it leverages existing resources in the economy. The suppliers are willing to give the new factory a commission or finder's fee because they don't have to do any marketing. They're willing to pay a premium in order to reach the ever-expanding roster of the new factory's membership. (That's why Apple is able to command a 30% fee for selling music, movies, and apps.)

By selling products and services produced by other companies, the new factory also takes advantage of the long tail strategy (see Chris Anderson's book *The Long Tail*). This means the new factory has a huge supply of products and yet doesn't need to worry which products sell and which don't. For example, Apple doesn't worry which song is a hit; it makes money no matter what. The same applies to Amazon. They don't care which book becomes a best-seller.

The one-stop store is a win-win for all three

parties: the members, the suppliers and the new factory. The members win because they have a single place to get everything they need. The suppliers win because they gain access to previously-hard-to-reach prospects, and the new factory wins because it generates passive income. The overall economy also benefits because the new factory generates demand for previously under-utilized resources.

THE OPEN MIND

One of the biggest problems with old factory thinking is that it closes your mind to potential opportunities. It stops you from imagining new ways to help people. It makes you egocentric and turns your mind into a closed fist.

New factory thinking and the new factory model, however, open the closed fist of your mind. The very bones of your company embody a customer-first philosophy. It sets your sights much higher and brings into action your best intentions. It allows you to demonstrate to prospects the value you provide without turning them off with a sales pitch. It also honors the relationship you have with your best customers by designating them as members. And finally, it maximizes your revenue potential by providing your members with a vast compendium of resources in a one-stop store.

The new factory is also structured to match the new conditions of the 21st Century marketplace: exponential change, convergent competition, and empowered consumers. Designed as a value hub, the new factory connects its network of members to its network of suppliers, and grows organically by continuously expanding the size of both networks. It adapts easily to changes in the marketplace because its core business anchors—its customer type and big idea—are future-proof. Operating within this model, the new factory is able to continuously expand its influence, its customer relationships, and its value propositions. That's why companies designed as new factories will prosper in the coming years while companies designed as old factories will falter.

BILL BISHOP

CHAPTER 8

FREE ENTERPRISE & DEMOCRACY

There is an inextricable link between democracy and free enterprise. The institutions of democracy are the foundation of a robust free enterprise system. So if you want to have a great business, you need to defend the pillars of democracy.

Unfortunately, this is a subject that confuses a lot of business people. They equate democracy with liberalism, and think that liberals are anti-business. This make them think that an authoritarian government is good for business.

So let's see if that holds up under scrutiny.

First, are liberals anti-business? That has not been my experience. I know many liberals who are excellent business people. They believe in free markets, capitalism and support the promotion of entrepreneurism. They don't want the government telling them what to do, and they don't want high taxes. But they also recognize that they have to accept a certain degree of regulation and taxes. They know that being part of a community comes with the territory of being a business owner.

Secondly, democracy is not about being a liberal, a conservative or a libertarian. Democracy is a playing field in which everyone participates under a set of agreed-upon rules. The key for everyone is to understand these rules and play fair within them.

So what are the rules of the democracy game?

One, everyone gets to say what they think. As long as their speech is not hateful or leads to a riot (like yelling fire in a movie theatre when there is no fire), anyone can say what they please. You might not like what someone says, but you defend their right to say it.

Two, we all protect and defend the electoral process. We do not try to subvert it or deny the right of anyone to cast their lawful vote. Furthermore, if we lose an election, we respect the result and work towards winning the next election.

Three, we do not allow any particular interest group to take control of the government or the electoral process. We don't let powerful special interests completely control the agenda of the government.

Four, we respect the rule of law. While we may work to change laws, we afford everyone a fair hearing in the courts of justice.

Of course, the story of democracy is much grander than my simple overview here. The point is that democracy is a sacred trust, and also the underpinning of capitalism and the success of your business.

That's why I encourage you to defend the fundamentals of our democracy. It doesn't matter if you are a Republican or a Democrat, a liberal or a conservative, a libertarian or socialist. Those are just matters of degree. Our common bond is that we respect the rules of democracy and we pledge to observe them.

For my part, I'm going to keep these thoughts in mind during the next four years. I will keep an eye on the Trump administration. I will ask: "Do their policies strengthen or undermine our democracy, and by extension support or undermine our capitalist system?"

I hope that the policies of the Trump administration lead to greater prosperity, not just in the short-term but in the long-term. I hope they keep taxes in line, but also lower the deficit and debt.

I also hope that they don't create a Trump

bubble that will burst like the financial crisis of 2008 under the last Republican government. I don't want just a few people to prosper under this government, I want everyone to prosper.

You can do your part. Speak up. Tell people what you think. If you believe what I've written is bilious nonsense, send me a email and tell me. If you are respectful in your opinion, I will read your comments and respond to them.

Speaking up is key to the success of our economy. In a society where everyone speaks their mind, more creative ideas are generated. When people feel free to speak honestly, more intelligence is gathered and more solutions are found. Creativity and intelligence leads to new products and services, and greater economic growth.

And forget about your political affiliation. Don't let being a Republican or a Democrat put you in a mental and ideological straitjacket. Nobody in the marketplace cares what party you belong to. If you provide them with value, they will buy your products and hire your services. Now is the time to free up your mind to help others: to grow your business.

While it might appear to many that Trump's economic and social policies are a step backwards, I take a different view. I believe the disruption caused by Donald Trump will actually speed up the end of the Industrial Revolution (the old factory in my parlance), and accelerate the emergence of the new factory economy. By dismantling the infrastructure of the old factory economy, built up over decades, they will create a vacuum that will be filled by the inexorable dictates of incentive-creativity and new factory thinking.

How you respond to the challenges and opportunities presented by the Trump administration will determine the success or failure of your business. Doing nothing or defending the status quo are not options. You need to Trump-Proof your business.

The time to start is right now. Best of luck.

Bill Bishop
January 2017

ABOUT THE AUTHOR

Bill Bishop is CEO of **The BIG Idea Company,** and the creator of **The BIG Idea Adventure** program. His team of coaches helps entrepreneurs around the world develop innovative BIG Ideas to grow their business.

He's the author of many business books, including **How To Sell A Lobster** (which has sold more than a million copies worldwide) and **The New Factory Thinker,** about how to succeed in a disrupted marketplace.

He's also the publisher of **BIG Idea Magazine,** about companies and individuals who are succeeding by disrupting the status quo in the marketplace.

Visit BishopBIGIdeas.com

To speak to Bill,
call 647.436.8829 x101

BIBLIOGRAPHY

Anderson, Chris. *Free: The Future of a Radical Price.* New York: Hyperion, 2009. Print.

Anderson, Chris. *The Long Tail: Why the Future of Business Is Selling Less of More.* New York: Hyperion, 2006. Print.

Berger, Warren. *A More Beautiful Question: The Power of Inquiry to Spark Breakthrough Ideas.* N.p.: n.p., n.d. Print.

Bishop, Bill. *Beyond Basketballs: The New Revolutionary Way to Build a Successful Business in a Post-product World.* Bloomington, IN: IUniverse, 2010. Print.

Bishop, Bill. *Global Marketing for the Digital Age.* Lincolnwood, IL: NTC Business, 1999. Print.

Bishop, Bill. *Going To The Net: Winning The Psychological Game Of Tennis.* New York: Amazon, 2014. Print.

Bishop, Bill. *How to Sell a Lobster: The Money-making Secrets of a Streetwise Entrepreneur.* Toronto: Key Porter, 2006. Print.

Bishop, Bill. *The Problem with Penguins: Stand out in a Crowded Marketplace by Packaging Your Big Idea.* S.l.: Iuniverse, 2010. Print.

Bishop, Bill. *The Strategic Enterprise: Growing a Business for the 21st Century.* Toronto: Stoddart, 2000. Print.

Bishop, Bill. *Strategic Marketing for the Digital Age.* Lincolnwood, Chicago, Illinois, USA: American Marketing Association, 1998. Print.

Brynjolfsson, Erik, and Andrew McAfee. *The Second Machine Age: Work, Progress, and Prosperity in a Time of Brilliant Technologies.* N.p.: n.p., n.d. Print.

Capra, Fritjof. *The Tao of Physics: An Exploration of the Parallels between Modern Physics and Eastern Mysticism.* Berkeley: Shambhala, 1975. Print.

Capra, Fritjov. *The Turning Point.* New York: Simon & Schuster, 1982. Print.

Carr, Nicholas G. *The Glass Cage: Automation and Us.* New York City: W.W. Norton, 2014. Print.

Catmull, Edwin E., and Amy Wallace. *Creativity, Inc.: Overcoming the Unseen Forces That Stand in the Way of True Inspiration.* N.p.: n.p., n.d. Print.

Cialdini, Robert B. *Influence: The Psychology of Persuasion.* New York: Collins, 2007. Print.

Diamandis, Peter H., and Steven Kotler. *Bold: How to Go Big, Achieve Success, and Impact the World.* N.p.: n.p., n.d. Print.

Diamond, Jared M. *Collapse: How Societies Choose to Fail or Succeed.* New York: Viking, 2005. Print.

Dixon, Matthew, and Brent Adamson. *The Challenger Sale: Taking Control of the Customer Conversation.* New York: Portfolio/Penguin, 2011. Print.

Doidge, Norman. *The Brain That Changes Itself: Stories of Personal Triumph from the Frontiers of Brain Science.* New York: Viking, 2007. Print.

Duhigg, Charles. *The Power of Habit: Why We Do What We Do in Life and Business.* New York: Random House, 2012. Print.

Eggers, William D., and Paul Macmillan. *The Solution Revolution: How Business, Government, and Social Enterprises Are Teaming up to Solve Society's Toughest Problems.* N.p.: n.p., n.d. Print.

Ferriss, Timothy. *The 4-hour Work Week: Escape 9-5, Live Anywhere, and Join the New Rich.* Chatham: Vermilion, 2011. Print.

Flynn, Anthony, Emily Flynn. Vencat, and Dennis C. Flynn. *Custom Nation: Why Customization Is the Future of Business and How to Profit from It.* Dallas, TX: BenBella, 2012. Print.

Friedman, Thomas L. *The World Is Flat: A Brief History of the Twenty-first Century.* New York: Farrar, Straus and Giroux, 2005. Print.

Godin, Seth. *Permission Marketing: Turning Strangers into Friends, and Friends into Customers.* New York: Simon & Schuster, 1999. Print.

Haidt, Jonathan. *The Happiness Hypothesis: Finding Modern Truth in Ancient Wisdom.* New York: Basic, 2006. Print.

Hanson, Rick, and Richard Mendius. *Buddha's Brain: The Practical Neuroscience of Happiness, Love & Wisdom.* Oakland, CA: New Harbinger Publications, 2009. Print.

Hanson, Rick. *Hardwiring Happiness: The New Brain Science of Contentment, Calm, and Confidence.* N.p.: n.p., n.d. Print.

Harnish, Verne. *Scaling Up: How a Few Companies Make It ... and Why the Rest Don't.* N.p.: n.p., n.d. Print.

Hawken, Paul, Amory B. Lovins, and L. Hunter Lovins. *Natural Capitalism: Creating the next Industrial Revolution.* Boston: Little, Brown, 1999. Print.

Heath, Chip, and Dan Heath. *Made to Stick: Why Some Ideas Survive and Others Die.* New York: Random House, 2007. Print.

Heath, Chip, and Dan Heath. *Made to Stick: Why Some Ideas Survive and Others Die.* New York: Random House, 2007. Print.

Heath, Chip, and Dan Heath. *Switch: How to Change Things When Change Is Hard.* New York: Broadway, 2010. Print.

Howe, Jeff. *Crowdsourcing: Why the Power of the Crowd Is Driving the Future of Business.* New York: Crown Business, 2008. Print.

Isaacson, Walter. *Steve Jobs.* New York: Simon & Schuster, 2011. Print.

Kondō, Marie, and Cathy Hirano. *The Life-changing Magic of Tidying Up: The Japanese Art of Decluttering and Organizing.* N.p.: n.p., n.d. Print.

Kurzweil, Ray. *The Singularity Is Near: When Humans Transcend Biology.* New York: Viking, 2005. Print.

Lanier, Jaron. *Who Owns the Future?* N.p.: n.p., n.d. Print.

Levitt, Theodore. *Marketing Myopia.* Boston, MA: Harvard Business, 2008. Print.

Lewis, David. *The Brain Sell: When Science Meets Shopping: How the New Mind Sciences and the Persuasion Industry Are Reading Our Thoughts, Influencing Our Emotions and Stimulating Us to Shop.* N.p.: Nicholas Brealey, n.d. Print.

Lietaer, Bernard A., and Jacqui Dunne. *Rethinking Money: How New Currencies Turn Scarcity into Prosperity.* San Francisco: Berrett-Koehler,

2013. Print.

Lowitt, Eric. *The Future of Value: How Sustainability Creates Value through Competitive Differentiation.* San Francisco: Jossey-Bass, 2011. Print.

McLuhan, Marshall. *The Medium Is the Message.* Corte Madera: Gingko Pr., 2005. Print.

Marchal, Lucie. *The Mesh.* New York: Appleton-Century-Crofts, 1949. Print.

Michelli, Joseph A. *The Starbucks Experience: 5 Principles for Turning Ordinary into Extraordinary.* New York: McGraw-Hill, 2007. Print.

Pine, B. Joseph., and James H. Gilmore. *The Experience Economy Work Is Theatre & Every Business a Stage.* Boston: Harvard Business School, 1999. Print.

Pink, Daniel H. *A Whole New Mind: Why Right-brainers Will Rule the Future.* New York: Riverhead, 2006. Print.

Putnam, Robert D. *Bowling Alone: The Collapse and Revival of American Community.* New York: Simon & Schuster, 2000. Print.

Ries, Eric. *The Lean Startup: How Today's Entrepreneurs Use Continuous Innovation to Create Radically Successful Businesses.* New York: Crown Business, 2011. Print.

Rifkin, Jeremy. *The Third Industrial Revolution: How*

Lateral Power Is Transforming Energy, the Economy, and the World. New York: Palgrave Macmillan, 2011. Print.

Rifkin, Jeremy. *Zero Marginal Cost Society: The Rise of the Collaborative Commons and the End of Capitalism.* N.p.: n.p., n.d. Print.

Snow, Richard. *I Invented the Modern Age: The Rise of Henry Ford.* New York: Simon & Schuster, n.d. Print.

Sommers, Sam. *Situations Matter: Understanding How Context Transforms Your World.* New York: Riverhead, 2011. Print.

Thaler, Richard H. *Misbehaving: The Making of Behavioural Economics.* London: Lane, 2015. Print.

Thomas, Martin. *Loose: The Future of Business Is Letting Go.* London: Headline, 2011. Print.

Toffler, Alvin, and Heidi Toffler. *Revolutionary Wealth.* New York: Knopf, 2006. Print.

Toffler, Alvin. *The Third Wave.* New York: Morrow, 1980. Print.

Wilber, Ken. *A Theory of Everything: An Integral Vision for Business, Politics, Science, and Spirituality.* Boston: Shambhala, 2000. Print.

Read *The New Factory Thinker*. Learn how to re-wire your mind for success in a disrupted marketplace. **Available at Amazon.com.**

You can also visit **newfactorythinker.com**

Read *How To Sell A Lobster*. This is Bill Bishop's top selling book. It has sold more than a million copies in more than 25 countries and has been translated into 12 languages. Learn unconventional strategies to make bigger sales at higher profit margins.
Available at Amazon.com.

What's your BIG Idea?

Schedule your FREE
BIG Idea Brainstorming Session today
During this free two-hour **creative session**, you and your team will use *New Factory Thinking* to create new BIG ideas for your business.

BIG Ideas can be:
- One-of-a-kind promotional concepts;
- New high-profit products and services;
- Innovative business models;
- New technologies and applications; and
- Completely new kinds of businesses.

To book your free BIG Idea session, call 647.436.8829 x10

Made in the USA
Lexington, KY
14 March 2017